HALLOWEEN
AD-LiBS

(FOR KIDS)

HERE ARE INSTRUCTIONS ON HOW TO PLAY AD LIBS:

GATHER A GROUP OF PLAYERS (2 OR MORE).
CHOOSE AN AD LIB STORY. THESE ARE PRE-WRITTEN STORIES
WITH BLANK SPACES FOR DIFFERENT PARTS OF SPEECH.
DESIGNATE ONE PLAYER AS THE "READER" WHO WILL ASK
FOR WORDS AND FILL IN THE BLANKS.
THE READER ASKS THE OTHER PLAYERS FOR SPECIFIC TYPES
OF WORDS TO FILL IN THE BLANKS, SUCH AS:

NOUNS (PERSON, PLACE, OR THING)
VERBS (ACTION WORDS)
ADJECTIVES (DESCRIPTIVE WORDS)
ADVERBS (WORDS THAT DESCRIBE VERBS)

PLAYERS PROVIDE WORDS WITHOUT KNOWING THE CONTEXT
OF THE STORY.
THE READER FILLS IN EACH BLANK WITH THE GIVEN WORDS.
ONCE ALL BLANKS ARE FILLED, THE READER READS THE
COMPLETED STORY ALOUD TO THE GROUP.
ENJOY THE OFTEN SILLY AND NONSENSICAL RESULT!
FOR ADDED FUN, YOU CAN TAKE TURNS BEING THE READER
FOR DIFFERENT STORIES.
REMEMBER, THE GOAL IS TO BE CREATIVE AND HAVE FUN.
THERE ARE NO WRONG ANSWERS!

EXAMPLE

BEFORE

"_____! We need to _____ to the party as
EXCLAMATION   VERB

_____ as possible. We only have _____ minutes to get
ADVERB ENDING IN "LY"   NUMBER

there." So we jumped in the _____ car and sped off.
                            ADJECTIVE

After the Story Teller fills in the blanks with words from the players

"___Yuck___! We need to ___dance___ to the party as
EXCLAMATION   VERB

___quietly___ as possible. We only have __900__ minutes to get
ADVERB ENDING IN "LY"   NUMBER

there." So we jumped in the __furry__ car and sped off.
                            ADJECTIVE

AFTER

SAMPLE WORDS

NOUNS:

ZOMBIE

TOMBSTONE

WITCH

CAULDRON

GHOST

PUMPKIN

VAMPIRE

WEREWOLF

SKELETON

BAT

VERBS:

CREEP

HOWL

HAUNT

CACKLE

LURK

SHRIEK

POSSESS

BEWITCH

SLITHER

CONJURE

ADJECTIVES:

SPOOKY

EERIE

GHASTLY

HAUNTED

CURSED

SINISTER

CREEPY

BLOODCURDLING

SHADOWY

MONSTROUS

THE HAUNTED HOUSE TOUR

1. ADJECTIVE _____
2. NAME _____
3. ADJECTIVE _____
4. OCCUPATION _____
5. ADVERB _____
6. UNPLEASANT SMELL _____
7. PLURAL NOUN _____
8. NOUN _____
9. ROOM IN A HOUSE _____
10. NUMBER _____
11. ANIMAL, PLURAL _____
12. VERB ENDING IN -ING _____
13. ANOTHER ROOM IN A HOUSE _____
14. MUSICAL INSTRUMENT _____
15. ADJECTIVE _____
16. BODY PART _____
17. VERB _____
18. ADJECTIVE _____
19. SPOOKY SOUND _____
20. COLOR _____
21. LAST NAME _____
22. ADJECTIVE _____
23. PIECE OF FURNITURE _____
24. VERB _____
25. CELEBRITY _____
26. HALLOWEEN COSTUME _____

THE HAUNTED HOUSE TOUR

On a _____ Halloween night, I joined a tour of the
      1.adjective

tour of the infamous _____ Manor. As we approached
               2. name

the _____ gates, our _____ guide greeted us
    3. adjective   *4. occupation*

with a _____ grin.
     5. adverb

The foyer smelled like _____ and was decorated with
          6. unpleasant smell

_____. Suddenly, a _____ flew past my head!
7. plural noun   *8. noun*

We entered the _____, where _____
      9. room in a house   *10. number*

_____ were _____ on the chandelier.
11. animal, plural   *12. verb ending in -ing*

In the _____, a ghostly figure played a _____.
13. another room in a house   *14. musical instrument*

The melody was so _____ that my _____ began to
        15. adjective   *16. body part*

_____.
  17. verb

As we climbed the _____ staircase, I heard _____
      18. adjective   *19. spooky sound*

coming from behind a _____ door. "That's Old Man
        20. color

_____," our guide whispered. The tour ended in the attic,
21. last name

where a _____ crystal ball sat on a _____.
    22. adjective   *23. piece of furniture*

When I _____ it, the ball revealed a vision of _____
   24. verb   *25. celebrity*

dressed as a _____.
    26. halloween costume

AD-LIBS

TRICK-OR-TREAT ADVENTURE

1. ADJECTIVE _____
2. OCCUPATION _____
3. NOUN _____
4. FAMILY MEMBER _____
5. ADJECTIVE _____
6. EMOTION _____
7. VERB, PAST TENSE _____
8. STREET NAME _____
9. PLURAL NOUN _____
10. COLOR _____
11. ADJECTIVE _____
12. ANIMAL _____
13. VERB _____
14. CELEBRITY _____
15. TYPE OF CANDY _____
16. ADJECTIVE _____
17. VERB _____
18. ADJECTIVE _____
19. SPOOKY SOUND _____
20. MYTHICAL CREATURE _____
21. ADJECTIVE _____
22. HALLOWEEN MONSTER _____
23. PLURAL NOUN _____
24. CONTAINER _____
25. WEATHER PHENOMENON _____
26. ADJECTIVE _____

TRICK-OR-TREAT ADVENTURE

On Halloween night, I dressed up as a _____ _____
                                        1. adjective   *2. occupation*
and grabbed my _____ to collect candy. My _____
                  3. noun   *4. family member*
warned me to be_____, but I was too _____ to care!
                  5. adjective   *6. emotion*
As I _____down _____ Street, I saw houses decorated
      7. verb, past tense   *8. street name*
with _____ and _____ lights. Suddenly, a _____
       9. plural noun   *10. color*   *11. adjective*
_____jumped out, making me_____! At the first house, a
12. animal   *13. verb*
_____ answered the door, offering _____. The next
14. Celebrity   *15. type of candy*
home had a _____ jack-o'-lantern that seemed to_____ at
             16. Adjective   *17. verb*
me. While crossing a _____bridge, I heard a_____.
                       18. adjective   *19. spooky sound*
 Was it the _____ rumored to haunt this neighborhood? My
              20. mythical creature
last stop was the _____ mansion on the hill. The owner,
                    21. adjective
dressed as a _____, handed out _____ instead of candy! As I
               22. Halloween monster   *23. plural noun*
headed home with my_____ full of treats, a chilly
                      24. container
_____made me shiver. What a _____Halloween
25. weather phenomenon   *26. adjective*
night it had been!

AD-LIBS

THE WITCH'S POTION RECIPE

1. ADJECTIVE _____
2. ADJECTIVE _____
3. NAME _____
4. VERB _____
5. NUMBER _____
6. PLURAL NOUN _____
7. COLOR _____
8. ADJECTIVE _____
9. BODY PART _____
10. ANIMAL _____
11. FOOD ITEM _____
12. PERSON _____
13. COLOR _____
14. VERB _____
15. NOUN _____
16. NONSENSE WORD _____
17. ADJECTIVE _____
18. PLANT _____
19. NUMBER _____
20. ADJECTIVE _____
21. ADVERB _____
22. SMELL _____
23. EMOTION _____
24. WEATHER PHENOMENON _____
25. NUMBER _____
26. PLURAL NOUN _____

THE WITCH'S POTION RECIPE

In a _____ forest, a _____ witch named _____
    1. adjective   *2. adjective*   *3. name*

stirred her cauldron. Tonight, she'd brew a potion to _____
                                                    4. verb

the entire town! She tossed in and a _____ _____
                                  5. number   *6. plural noun*

handful of _____ dust. "Now for the secret ingredients," she
             7. color

cackled, reaching for her _____ spell book.
                           8. adjective

First, she added the _____ of a _____. Then, she
                   9. body part   *10. animal*

sprinkled in _____ powder and _____ tears. The
             11. food item   *12. person*

mixture turned _____ and began to _____. _____ waved
             13. color   *14. verb*   *3. name*

her _____ over the brew, chanting "_____!"
    15. noun   *16. nonsense word*

three times. She dropped in a _____ _____ and stirred
                           17. adjective   *18. plant*

_____ times clockwise with her _____ wand.
  19. number   *20. adjective*

The potion bubbled _____, releasing a _____ scent. To
                 21. adverb   *22. smell*

finish, she added a pinch of _____ and a dash of _____.
                    23. emotion   *24. weather phenomenon*

As the clock struck _____, the witch bottled her concoction.
             25. number

She cackled, imagining the townspeople's _____
                                    26. plural noun

transforming at midnight.

Little did she know, her spell would backfire, turning her into a
_____ instead!
10. animal

AD-LIBS
THE MYSTERIOUS PUMPKIN PATCH

1. ADJECTIVE_____

2. NAME_____

3. LAST NAME_____

4. COLOR_____

5. ADJECTIVE_____

6. VEGETABLE_____

7. VERB_____

8. PLURAL NOUN_____

9. VERB ENDING IN -ING_____

10. ADVERB_____

11. BODY PART_____

12. ADJECTIVE_____

13. NOUN_____

14. ADJECTIVE_____

15. NUMBER_____

16. PLURAL NOUN_____

17. VERB_____

18. NUMBER_____

19. ANIMALS_____

20. VERB ENDING IN -ING_____

21. COLOR_____

22. VERB_____

23. NOUN_____

24. ADVERB_____

25. ADJECTIVE_____

26. NOUN_____

THE MYSTERIOUS PUMPKIN PATCH

On a _____ October evening, _____ visited Farmer
     1. adjective   *2. name*

_____'s pumpkin patch. The _____ moon cast eerie
 3. last name   *4. color*

shadows as _____ searched for the perfect _____ pumpkin.
        2. name   *5. adjective*

Suddenly, a _____ began to _____. Startled, _____
      6. vegetable   *7. verb*   *2. name*

stumbled backward into a pile of _____. The pumpkins
              8. plural noun

Started _____, their vines _____ wrapping around
  9. verb ending in -ing   *10. adverb*

_____'s _____.
 2. name   *11. body part*

A _____ scarecrow came to life, its _____ head
 12. adjective   *13. noun*

bobbing as it spoke: "To escape, solve my _____ riddle!"
              14. adjective

The riddle was: "What has _____ _____ but can't _____?"
     15. number *16. plural noun*   *17. verb*

While pondering, _____ noticed _____ _____
      2. name   *18. number* *19. animals*

_____ nearby. Their _____ eyes glowed in the darkness.
20. verb ending in -ing   *21. color*

Just as _____ was about to _____, the answer came:
   2. name   *22. verb*

"_____!" The vines retreated, and the pumpkins returned to
 23. noun

normal. Relieved, _____ quickly chose a pumpkin and
       2. name

_____ left the patch. At home, while carving, _____ found
24. adverb   *2. name*

a _____ _____ inside – a reminder of the mysterious
 25. adjective   *26. noun*

adventure.

THE GHOST'S SPOOKY TALE

1. ADJECTIVE_____
2. ADJECTIVE_____
3. NAME_____
4. ROOM IN A HOUSE_____
5. NUMBER_____
6. VERB_____
7. ADJECTIVE_____
8. NUMBER_____
9. PLURAL NOUN_____
10. ADJECTIVE_____
11. ADVERB_____
12. OCCUPATION_____
13. COLOR_____
14. EXCLAMATION_____
15. VERB, PAST TENSE_____
16. VERB_____
17. OBJECT_____
18. BODY PART_____
19. ADJECTIVE_____
20. ANIMAL_____
21. HALLOWEEN COSTUME_____
22. VERB_____
23. SILLY PHRASE_____

THE GHOST'S SPOOKY TALE

In a _____ old mansion, a _____ ghost named
      1. adjective   *2. adjective*

_____ floated through the _____ . For _____
   3. name   *4. room in a house*   *5. number*

years, ____ had been trying to ____ the living, but always failed.
      3. name   *6. verb*

One Halloween night, a group of _____ _____
                            8. Number   *9. plural noun*

entered the mansion. _____ saw an opportunity to be _____
               3. name   *10. adjective*

at last!

The ghost _____ approached the first person, a _____
         11. adverb   *12. occupation*

wearing a _____ costume. _____ wailed, "_____ !"
        13. color   *3. name*   *14. exclamation*

but the person just _____ .
         15. verb, past tense

Frustrated, _____ tried to _____ a _____ , but it went
        3. name   *16. verb*   *17. object*

right through. The ghost's _____ drooped in disappointment.
            18. body part

Suddenly, a _____ _____ appeared, wearing a _____ .
     19. adjective *20. animal*   *21. Halloween costume*

To _____ 's surprise, it could see the ghost!
   3. name

The _____ spoke, "To be seen, you must _____ three times
  20. animal   *22. verb*

and say '_____ '."
   23. silly phrase

_____ did as instructed, and suddenly became visible! The
 3. name

_____ gasped in amazement.
9. plural noun

AD-LIBS

A NIGHT AT THE HAUNTED CARNIVAL

1. NAME_____
2. ADJECTIVE_____
3. NUMBER_____
4. COLOR_____
5. PLURAL NOUN_____
6. ADJECTIVE_____
7. PLURAL NOUN_____
8. VERB_____
9. ADVERB_____
10. MYTHICAL CREATURES_____
11. ADJECTIVE_____
12. VERB_____
13. ANIMAL, PLURAL_____
14. ADJECTIVE_____
15. NOUN_____
16. VERB ENDING IN -ING_____
17. NUMBER_____
18. PLURAL OBJECT_____
19. ADJECTIVE_____
20. OCCUPATION_____
21. NOUN_____
22. EXCLAMATION_____
23. PLURAL NOUN_____
24. VERB_____
25. ADJECTIVE_____
26. HOLIDAY_____

A NIGHT AT THE HAUNTED CARNIVAL

On Halloween, _____ visited the _____ carnival that
　　　　　　　1. name　　　　　　　　　*2. adjective*
mysteriously appeared in town. The entrance was adorned with
_____ _____ _____, creating an eerie atmosphere.
3. number　　*4. color*　　*5. plural noun*
The first attraction was a _____ funhouse. Inside, _____
　　　　　　　　　　　　　6. adjective　　　　　　　*1. name*
encountered a room full of _____ that seemed to _____. In the
　　　　　　　　　　　　　7. plural noun　　　　　　　*8. verb*
mirror maze, reflections _____ transformed into _____.
　　　　　　　　　　9. adverb　　　　　　　*10. mythical creatures*
Next, _____ rode the _____ Ferris wheel. At the top,
　　　1. name　　　　　　*11. adjective*
the seat began to _____, nearly causing _____ to fall into a
　　　　　　　12. verb　　　　　　　　　*1. name*
pit of _____ below.
　　　13. animal, plural
At the carnival games, _____ won a _____ _____
　　　　　　　　　　1. name　　　　　　*14. adjective*　*15. noun*
by _____ _____ _____. The prize felt
16. verb ending in -ing　*17. number*　*18. plural object*
oddly _____ to touch.
　　19. adjective
The final stop was the fortune teller's tent. The mystic, dressed as a
_____, gazed into a _____ and exclaimed,"_____!
20. occupation　　　　　　*21. noun*　　　　　　*22. exclamation*
I see _____ in your future!"
　　　23. plural noun
Suddenly, the carnival began to _____. As _____ rushed to
　　　　　　　　　　　　24. verb　　　*1. name*
the exit, a _____ clown appeared, whispering, "See you next
　　　25. adjective
_____!"
26. holiday

AD-LIBS

THE VAMPIRE'S COSTUME PARTY

1. NAME_____
2. ADJECTIVE_____
3. ADJECTIVE_____
4. ADJECTIVE_____
5. NUMBER_____
6. COLOR_____
7. PLURAL NOUN_____
8. OCCUPATION_____
9. ADJECTIVE_____
10. LIQUID_____
11. CONTAINER, PLURAL_____
12. MUSICAL INSTRUMENT_____
13. MYTHICAL CREATURE_____
14. VERB, PAST TENSE_____
15. FOOD_____
16. ADJECTIVE_____
17. BODY PART_____
18. ADJECTIVE_____
19. VERB, PAST TENSE_____
20. ANIMAL_____
21. OBJECT_____
22. ADJECTIVE_____
23. PROFESSION_____
24. NOUN_____

THE VAMPIRE'S COSTUME PARTY

Count _____, a _____ vampire, decided to host a
     1. name   *2. adjective*

_____ Halloween costume party at his _____ castle.
3. adjective   *4. adjective*

He sent out _____ invitations on _____ bat-shaped cards.
        5. number   *6. color*

On the night of the party, guests arrived dressed as various _____.
                                      7. plural noun

The Count, ironically, wore a _____ costume. His_____
                 8. occupation   *9. adjective*

butler, Igor, greeted everyone with a tray of _____served in
                            10. liquid

_____.
11. container, plural

The party featured a_____ player who was actually a
         12. musical instrument

_____ in disguise. Guests _____ to the beat while
13. mythical creature   *14. verb, past tense*

while snacking on _____eyeballs and _____fingers.
       15. food   *16. adjective*

During a game of "Pin the _____ on the Werewolf," a _____
          17. body part   *18. adjective*

witch accidentally _____her wand, turning the Count's pet
      19. verb, past tense

_____into a_____.
  20. animal   *21. object*

The highlight of the evening was a_____ costume contest.
                     22. adjective

The winner, dressed as a_____, received a trophy shaped
           23. profession

like a _____.
  24. noun

AD-LIBS
THE WEREWOLF'S FULL MOON NIGHT

1. ADJECTIVE _____

2. NAME _____

3. SENSATION _____

4. COLOR _____

5. BODY PART _____

6. ADJECTIVE _____

7. ADJECTIVE _____

8. NUMBER _____

9. PLURAL NOUN _____

10. COLOR _____

11. VERB, PAST TENSE _____

12. OCCUPATION _____

13. OBJECT _____

14. ADVERB _____

15. FOOD ITEM _____

16. VERB _____

17. ADJECTIVE _____

18. PLURAL NOUN _____

19. ADJECTIVE _____

20. BUILDING _____

21. HALLOWEEN CREATURES _____

22. VERB ENDING IN -ING _____

THE WEREWOLF'S FULL MOON NIGHT

On a _____ Halloween night _____ felt a familiar
　　　1. adjective　　　　　　　　　*2. name*

_____ as the _____ full moon rose. Hair sprouted from
3. sensation　　　　*4. color*

their _____ as they transformed into a _____ werewolf.
　　5. body part　　　　　　　　　　　　　*6. adjective*

_____ bounded through the _____ forest, passing
2. name　　　　　　　　　　　　　　*7. adjective*

_____ _____ along the way. Their _____ eyes
8. number　　*9. plural noun*　　　　　　　　　　*10. color*

gleamed in the moonlight as they _____ over fallen logs.
　　　　　　　　　　　　　　11. verb, past tense

Suddenly, they encountered a _____ holding a_____.
　　　　　　　　　　　　12. occupation　　　　*13. object*

The person _____ offered _____ a _____,
　　　14. adverb　　　　　*2. name*　　*15. food item*

unaware of their true nature.

Resisting the urge to_____, _____ instead let out a
　　　　　　　16. verb　　*2. name*

_____ howl. The startled _____ dropped their _____
17. adjective　　　　　　　　*12. occupation*　　　　　*13. object*

and fled, leaving behind a trail of _____. _____
　　　　　　　　　　　　　　18. plural noun　　*2. name*

continued their nocturnal adventure, racing past a _____
　　　　　　　　　　　　　　　　　　　　19. adjective

graveyard and a _____. They even scared a group of
　　　20. building

_____ who were _____ nearby.
21. Halloween creatures　　*22. verb ending in -ing*

THE SKELETON'S DANCE PARTY

1. ADJECTIVE _____
2. PLURAL NOUN _____
3. ADJECTIVE _____
4. ADJECTIVE _____
5. NAME _____
6. ADVERB _____
7. BODY PART _____
8. ADJECTIVE _____
9. MUSICAL INSTRUMENT, PLURAL _____
10. VERB _____
11. VERB _____
12. BODY PART _____
13. ADJECTIVE _____
14. ADJECTIVE _____
15. NOUN _____
16. BODY PART _____
17. ADJECTIVE _____
18. VERB ENDING IN -ING _____
19. ADJECTIVE _____
20. VERB _____

THE SKELETON'S DANCE PARTY

Deep in a _____ graveyard, the _____were having
      1. adjective   *2. plural noun*

a _____dance party. The host, a tall _____ skeleton
   3. adjective   *4. adjective*

named_____, greeted his guests with a _____wave of his
   5. name   *6. adverb*

_____.
  7. body part

The _____ music was provided by a band of _____
   8. adjective   *9. musical instrument, plural*

players. Skeletons _____ and _____across the dance floor,
           11. verb   *11. verb*

their _____ rattling to the_____ beat.
   12. body part   *13. adjective*

Suddenly, a _____ witch arrived, cackling as she floated
    14. adjective

past the_____. "Who wants their _____ read?" she
    15. noun   *16. body part*

cried, holding up a _____ crystal ball.
17. adjective

_____ the skeleton cut in, _____ his date, a
  5. name   *18. verb ending in -ing*

_____ vampire. They _____ the night away, their
19. adjective   *20. verb*

shadows dancing on the _____ gravestones.
          1. adjective

As the clock struck midnight, the skeletons joined hands and

_____ in a _____ circle. Their joyful _____
11. verb   *13. adjective*   *17. adjective*

laughter echoed through the graveyard, making the living shiver
with delight.

AD-LIBS
THE MONSTER'S HALLOWEEN BASH

1. ADJECTIVE _____

2. ADJECTIVE _____

3. ADJECTIVE _____

4. MONSTER _____

5. EMOTION _____

6. PLURAL NOUN _____

7. LIQUID _____

8. CONTAINER, PLURAL _____

9. MUSICAL INSTRUMENT, PLURAL _____

10. ADJECTIVE _____

11. VERB _____

12. ADJECTIVE _____

13. VERB _____

14. ADJECTIVE _____

15. BODY PART _____

16. ADJECTIVE _____

17. ADJECTIVE _____

18. ADJECTIVE _____

19. PRIZE _____

20. ADJECTIVE _____

THE MONSTER'S HALLOWEEN BASH

The _____ creatures of the night were gathered for the
    1. adjective

_____ Monster's Halloween Bash. The host, a _____
  2. adjective   *3. adjective*

_____, greeted his guests with a _____ howl.
  4. monster   *5. emotion*

Vampires, witches, and _____ mingled, sipping _____
                           6. plural noun   *7. liquid*

from _____. A band of _____ played a _____
  8. container, plural   *9. musical instrument, plural*   *10. adjective*

melody as the monsters_____ across the dance floor.
                             11. verb

Suddenly, a _____ zombie stumbled in, moaning, "Brains!"
      12. adjective

The other monsters _____ in amusement.
                 13. verb

A _____ werewolf showed off its _____ moves,
  14. adjective   *15. body part*

narrowly avoiding a _____ chandelier that swung
              16. adjective

overhead. Meanwhile, a _____ mummy entered a
                  17. adjective

_____ costume contest, hoping to win the _____.
  18. adjective   *19. prize*

As the night wore on, the monsters continued to party and
_____ until the first rays of dawn crept over the horizon.
  11. verb

Reluctantly, they bid each other farewell, already looking forward
to next year's _____ Halloween bash!
           20. adjective

AD-LIBS
THE ENCHANTED BROOMSTICK RIDE

1.   ADJECTIVE_____

2.   NAME_____

3.   ADJECTIVE_____

4.   ADJECTIVE_____

5.   VERB_____

6.   ADJECTIVE_____

7.   PLURAL NOUN_____

8.   COLOR_____

9.   VERB_____

10. VERB_____

11. ADJECTIVE_____

12. SPOOKY STRUCTURE_____

13. VERB_____

14. ADJECTIVE_____

15. ADJECTIVE_____

16. HALLOWEEN CREATURES_____

17. VERB ENDING IN -ING_____

18. ADJECTIVE_____

19. ADJECTIVE_____

20. EMOTION_____

THE ENCHANTED BROOMSTICK RIDE

On a _____ Halloween night, the _____ witch climbed
   1. adjective   *2. name*

onto her _____ broomstick for a _____ ride. She_____ over
      3. adjective   *4. adjective*   *5. verb*

the _____ town, admiring the _____ carved into the
    6. adjective   *7. plural noun*

_____ pumpkins below.
   8. color

Suddenly, her broomstick _____ out of control! _____
                      9. verb   *2. name*

held on tight as it _____ through the _____ sky, past
            10. verb   *11. adjective*

a _____.
12. spooky structure

"Slow down!" she cried, but the broomstick _____ even faster.
                                 13. verb

_____ noticed a _____ cat scurrying across a
   2. name   *14. adjective*

_____ rooftop, then a group of _____
15. adjective   *16. Halloween creatures*

_____
17. verb ending in -ing

in a _____ graveyard. Finally, the broomstick came to a
     18. adjective

stop in a _____ forest clearing. _____ stumbled off,
      19. adjective   *2. name*

_____ but unharmed. As she dusted off her _____
  20. emotion   *3. adjective*

dress, the witch heard a _____ voice behind her. "Welcome
                   11. adjective

to my enchanted domain!" it cackled. This was going to be one
_____Halloween night.
    4. adjective

AD-LIBS
THE GHOSTLY SLEEPOVER

1. TIME OF DAY_____
2. NAME_____
3. PLURAL NOUN_____
4. ADJECTIVE_____
5. ADJECTIVE_____
6. ADJECTIVE_____
7. SUPERNATURAL BEING_____
8. EXCLAMATION_____
9. VERB, PAST TENSE_____
10. ADJECTIVE_____
11. NAME_____
12. PLURAL NOUN_____
13. ROOM IN A HOUSE_____
14. ADJECTIVE_____
15. COLOR_____
16. SPOOKY SOUND_____
17. VERB_____
18. ADJECTIVE_____
19. EMOTION_____
20. PLURAL NOUN_____

THE GHOSTLY SLEEPOVER

It was _____ when_____ and their _____
    1. time of day   *2. name*   *3. plural noun*
arrived at the _____ mansion for a spooky Halloween
           4. adjective
sleepover.

As they approached the _____ doors, a _____
             5. adjective   *6. adjective*
_____ appeared, moaning, "_____!" The friends
7. supernatural being   *8. exclamation*
_____ in fright, then realized it was just the _____
9. verb, past tense   *10. adjective*
butler, _____, playing a prank.
      11. name
Once inside, the group set up their _____ in the _____
              12. plural noun   *13. room in a house*
_____ turned on their _____ flashlight, casting eerie
   2. name   *14. adjective*
shadows on the _____ walls.
        15. color
Suddenly, a _____ echoed through the halls. The friends
      16. spooky sound
_____ under their _____, shivering. _____
   17. verb   *12. plural noun*   *11. name*
reappeared, laughing, "It's just the _____ wind!"
             17. adjective
As midnight approached, the friends told _____ ghost
            18. adjective
stories, their eyes wide with _____. Finally, they drifted off
          19. emotion
to sleep, dreaming of _____ and other Halloween
       20. plural noun
delights.

AD-LIBS

THE HAUNTED FOREST HIKE

1. ADJECTIVE_____
2. NAME_____
3. ADJECTIVE_____
4. COLOR_____
5. ADJECTIVE_____
6. BODY PART_____
7. SOUND_____
8. ANIMAL, PLURAL_____
9. PLURAL NOUN_____
10. TYPE OF PLANT_____
11. SPOOKY SOUND_____
12. VERB_____
13. ADJECTIVE_____
14. SUPERNATURAL BEING_____
15. ADJECTIVE_____
16. ADJECTIVE_____
17. EXCLAMATION_____
18. ADJECTIVE_____
19. BODY PART_____
20. VERB_____

THE HAUNTED FOREST HIKE

On a _____ autumn day, _____ decided to take a hike
      1. adjective   *2. name*

through the _____ forest. As they entered the _____
        3. adjective   *4. color*

woods, an _____feeling crept up their _____.
      5. adjective   *6. body part*

The _____ of _____ echoed all around. _____
    7. sound   *8. animal, plural*   *2. name*

quickened their pace, avoiding _____ and _____
                      9. plural noun   *10. type of plant*

that seemed to reach out and grab them.

Suddenly, _____ heard a _____ in the distance.
      2. name   *11. spooky sound*

Curiosity getting the better of them, they _____ towards the
                                12. verb

noise. In a _____ clearing, they came upon a _____
        13. adjective   *14. supernatural being*

dancing around a _____ fire.
           15. adjective

The _____ noticed _____ and let out a _____ cackle.
14. supernatural being   *2. name*   *16. adjective*

"_____!" it shouted, "You've stumbled upon my _____
17. exclamation   *18. adjective*

lair!"

_____ turned to flee, but their _____ felt heavy, as if
  2. name   *19. body part*

the forest itself was trying to _____ them.
                   20. verb

Just then, a _____ owl hooted, startling the _____.
       1. adjective   *14. supernatural being*

_____ seized the opportunity and quickly made their way
  2. name

back to the trail, heart pounding.

Back home, they vowed never to hike in the haunted forest alone
again.

THE WITCH'S LOST SPELL BOOK

1. NAME _____

2. ADJECTIVE _____

3. ADJECTIVE _____

4. ADJECTIVE _____

5. ADJECTIVE _____

6. ADJECTIVE _____

7. PLURAL NOUN _____

8. OBJECT, PLURAL _____

9. SOUND _____

10. ROOM IN A HOUSE _____

11. ADJECTIVE _____

12. PIECE OF FURNITURE _____

13. EXCLAMATION _____

14. ADJECTIVE _____

15. VERB _____

16. BODY PART _____

17. COLOR _____

18. SOUND _____

THE WITCH'S LOST SPELL BOOK

_____, a powerful _____ witch, couldn't find her trusty
1. name   *2. adjective*

_____ spell book anywhere. She frantically searched her
3. adjective

_____ cottage, muttering _____ curses under her breath.
4. adjective   *5. adjective*

"Where is that _____ book?" _____ cried, tossing _____
                        6. adjective   *1. name*   *7. plural noun*

and _____ aside. Suddenly, she heard a _____ coming
              8. object, plural   *9. sound*

from her _____.
                  10. room in a house

Cautiously, the witch entered to find her _____ black cat
                                                                  11. adjective

batting at the spell book, which had fallen open on the _____.
                                                                            12. piece of furniture

"_____!" she scolded, snatching up the tome.
13. exclamation

As _____ flipped through the pages, a _____ spell
        1. name   *14. adjective*

caught her eye. "Aha! This is just what I need to _____ my
                                                                          15. verb

missing wand," she declared.

The witch began chanting the incantation, waving her _____
                                                                              16. body part

in the air. A _____ mist swirled around the room, and with a
                      17. color

_____, the wand appeared in her hand.
18. sound

_____ smiled triumphantly, relieved to have her_____
1. name   *3. adjective*

spell book and _____ back.
                        16. body part

THE GOBLIN'S TRICK-OR-TREAT HEIST

1. TIME OF DAY_____
2. NAME_____
3. ADJECTIVE_____
4. HALLOWEEN COSTUME_____
5. ADJECTIVE_____
6. PLURAL NOUN_____
7. EXCLAMATION_____
8. VERB_____
9. COLOR_____
10. HALLOWEEN CREATURE_____
11. VERB_____
12. ADJECTIVE_____
13. VERB_____
14. HOLIDAY PHRASE_____
15. OCCUPATION_____
16. VERB_____
17. CONTAINER_____
18. TYPE OF CANDY_____
19. VERB_____
20. NUMBER_____

THE GOBLIN'S TRICK-OR-TREAT HEIST

It was _____ on Halloween night when the mischievous
       1. time of day

_____ the goblin set out to pull off the ultimate _____
   2. name   *3. adjective*

trick-or-treat heist.

Dressed as a _____, _____ crept through the
          4. Halloween costume   *2. name*

_____ neighborhood, eyeing the _____ piled high
5. adjective   *6. plural noun*

on porches. "_____," they snickered, "This is going to be easy!"
       7. exclamation

First, _____ _____ a _____ pillowcase from an
   2. name   *8. verb*   *9. color*

unsuspecting _____. Then, they _____ up to a _____
      10. Halloween creature   *11. verb*   *12. adjective*

house and _____ the door, shouting "_____!"
     13. verb   *14. holiday phrase*

When the _____ homeowner answered, _____ quickly
    15. occupation   *2. name*

_____ the entire _____ of _____ into their
16. verb   *17. container*   *18. type of candy*

pillowcase. They _____ down the street, cackling with glee.
     19. verb

As dawn approached, _____ counted their _____ haul,
       2. name   *6. plural noun*

which included _____ king-size chocolate bars! The greedy
      20. number

goblin had pulled off the ultimate Halloween heist.

Satisfied with their loot, _____ settled in for a_____
           2. name   *3. adjective*

sugar-filled day, already planning next year's trick-or-treat
adventure.

THE SPOOKY GRAVEYARD MYSTERY

1. ADJECTIVE_____
2. NAME_____
3. ADJECTIVE_____
4. ADJECTIVE_____
5. COLOR_____
6. ADJECTIVE_____
7. SPOOKY SOUND_____
8. SUPERNATURAL BEING_____
9. COLOR_____
10. SOUND_____
11. BODY PART_____
12. ADJECTIVE_____
13. ADJECTIVE_____
14. SENSATION_____
15. ADJECTIVE_____
16. PLURAL NOUN_____

THE SPOOKY GRAVEYARD MYSTERY

On a _____ Halloween night, _____ decided to
      1. adjective   *2. name*
investigate the_____ graveyard at the edge of town. Armed
           3. adjective
with a _____ flashlight, they cautiously approached the _____
      4. adjective   *5. color*
wrought-iron gates.
As _____ stepped between the _____ gravestones, a
     2. name   *6. adjective*
_____ made them jump. They shone their light on a _____
7. spooky sound   *8. supernatural being*
 emerging from the _____ mist.
                    9. color
"Wh-who are you?" _____ stammered. The _____
                    2. name   *8. supernatural being*
let out a _____ and pointed a _____ towards a _____
      10. sound   *11. body part*   *12. adjective*
crypt.
Curiosity overcoming fear, _____ slowly approached the
                       2. name
_____ crypt. They noticed a _____ symbol carved
12. adjective   *13. adjective*
into the door and felt a _____ wash over them.
                 14. sensation
Suddenly, the crypt door creaked open, revealing a _____
                                15. adjective
 treasure chest. _____ carefully lifted the lid, gasping at the
             2. name
_____ inside.
16. plural noun

.

AD-LIBS
THE HALLOWEEN COSTUME CONTEST

1. ADJECTIVE _____
2. NAME _____
3. ADJECTIVE _____
4. LOCATION _____
5. SUPERNATURAL BEINGS _____
6. PRIZE _____
7. ADJECTIVE _____
8. ADJECTIVE _____
9. PLURAL NOUN _____
10. NOUN _____
11. EMOTION _____
12. EXCLAMATION _____
13. ADJECTIVE _____
14. SOUND _____
15. SUPERNATURAL BEING _____
16. ADJECTIVE _____
17. ADJECTIVE _____
18. ADJECTIVE _____
19. ADJECTIVE _____

THE HALLOWEEN COSTUME CONTEST

It was the night of the annual _____ Halloween costume
                                        1. adjective
contest, and _____ couldn't wait to show off their _____
                  2. name   *3. adjective*
outfit.

As they arrived at the _____, ghosts, goblins, and _____
                              4. location   *5. supernatural beings*
were already gathered, each hoping to win the grand _____.
                                                              6. prize
_____ admired the creative costumes, from a _____
   2. name   *7. adjective*
vampire to a _____ werewolf. A group of _____
                   8. adjective   *9. plural noun*
was dressed as a _____.
                      10. noun
When it was _____'s turn to strut their stuff, the judges were
                  2. name
_____ by their _____ costume. "_____!"
   11. emotion   *3. adjective*   *12. exclamation*
they cried, "That's the _____ Halloween costume we've ever
                              13. adjective
seen!" The crowd erupted in _____, cheering for _____.
                                  14. sound   *2. name*
  As they accepted the _____, a _____ in a_____.
                            6.prize   *15. supernatural being*   *16. adjective*
mask approached, offering_____ a_____ treat.
                              2. name   *17. adjective*
"Congratulations," the _____ said in a _____ voice.
                            15. supernatural being   *18. adjective*
"But be careful - the night is young, and _____ tricks may be
                                                   19. adjective
in store."

AD-LIBS
THE CREEPY CANDY QUEST

1. TIME OF DAY_____
2. NAME_____
3. ADJECTIVE_____
4. ADJECTIVE_____
5. ADJECTIVE_____
6. HOLIDAY PHRASE_____
7. OCCUPATION_____
8. NUMBER_____
9. TYPE OF CANDY_____
10. ADJECTIVE_____
11. SUPERNATURAL BEING_____
12. SOUND_____
13. DEMAND_____
14. ADJECTIVE_____
15. TYPE OF CANDY_____
16. CONTAINER_____
17. ADJECTIVE_____
18. ADJECTIVE_____
19. NUMBER_____
20. TYPE OF CANDY_____

THE CREEPY CANDY QUEST

It was _____ on Halloween when _____ set out on a
      1. time of day   *2. name*

_____ candy quest. Armed with a [4. adjective] pillowcase,
3. adjective

they approached the first _____ house.
                   5. adjective

Knocking on the door, _____ shouted "_____!" A
              2. name   *6. holiday phrase*

_____ answered, dropping _____ _____ into their bag.
7. occupation   *8. number 9. type of candy*

As _____ continued down the _____ street, they
   2. name   *10. adjective*

noticed a _____ lurking in the shadows. The _____ let
    11. supernatural being   *11. supernatural being*

out a _____ and demanded "_____!"
   12. sound   *13. demand*

Not wanting any _____ trouble, _____ quickly dropped
        14. adjective   *2. name*

a _____ into the _____'s _____.
 15. type of candy   *11. supernatural being*   *16. container*

Satisfied, the _____ vanished into the _____ night.
   11. supernatural being   *17. adjective*

_____ hurried to the next house, where a _____ witch
2. name   *18. adjective*

cackled, "Trick or treat!" They happily accepted the _____
                             19. number

pieces of _____ she offered.
    20. type of candy

By the end of the night, _____'s pillowcase was overflowing
              2. name

with all sorts of _____ and_____. Their creepy candy
   9. type of candy   *20. type of candy*

quest had been a sweet success!

AD-LIBS
THE JACK-O'-LANTERN'S SECRET

1. ADJECTIVE_____
2. NAME_____
3. ADJECTIVE_____
4. ADJECTIVE_____
5. PLACE_____
6. VERB_____
7. SOUND_____
8. ADJECTIVE_____
9. NOUN_____
10. VERB, PAST TENSE_____
11. VERB_____
12. COLOR_____
13. VERB_____
14. ADJECTIVE_____
15. NOUN_____
16. PLACE_____
17. EMOTION_____
18. NOUN_____
19. ITEM_____
20. TYPE OF CREATURE_____

THE JACK-O'-LANTERN'S SECRET

On a _____ Halloween night, _____ decided to carve a
   1. Adjective   *2. name*

_____ jack-o'-lantern. They chose a _____ pumpkin
3. adjective   *4. adjective*

from the _____ and brought it home. As they began to _____
      5. place   *6. verb*

the top off, they heard a faint_____.
                         7. sound

Startled, _____ peered inside the pumpkin and gasped. Hidden
        2. name

within was a _____ _____! They carefully _____
      8. adjective   *9. noun*   *10. verb, past tense*

it out and examined it closely. The object seemed to _____
                                           11. verb

with an eerie _____ glow.
          12. color

Suddenly, the _____ began to_____, revealing a
          9. noun   *13. verb*

_____ message. It spoke of an ancient _____ buried
14. adjective   *15. noun*

beneath the _____ cemetery. _____'s heart raced with
        16. place   *2. name*

_____ as they realized they had stumbled upon a Halloween
17. emotion

_____.
   18. noun

Without hesitation, they grabbed their _____ and set off into
                              19. item

the night. As they approached the cemetery gates, a _____
                                    20. type of creature

emerged from the shadows. _____ knew their Halloween
                       2. name

adventure was just beginning.

THE PUMPKIN CARVING CONTEST

1. TOWN NAME _____
2. NAME _____
3. OCCUPATION _____
4. ADJECTIVE _____
5. VERB _____
6. TOOL _____
7. TIME OF DAY _____
8. ANOTHER NAME _____
9. ADJECTIVE _____
10. SUPERNATURAL CREATURE _____
11. VERB _____
12. BODY PART _____
13. NUMBER _____
14. PLURAL NOUN _____
15. ADJECTIVE _____
16. NOUN _____
17. PLURAL HALLOWEEN CHARACTER _____
18. VERB _____
19. EMOTION _____
20. ADJECTIVE _____

THE PUMPKIN CARVING CONTEST

The annual _____ Halloween pumpkin carving contest was
       1.town name

in full swing. _____, a _____ by day and pumpkin
       2. name   *3. occupation*

enthusiast by night, was determined to win. They selected a
_____ pumpkin and began to _____ it with their trusty
4. adjective   *5. verb*

_____.
   6. tool

As the _____ approached, _____ noticed their neighbor,
    7. time of day   *2. name*

_____, creating a suspiciously _____ design.
8. another name   *9. adjective*

Suddenly, a _____ appeared, offering to _____
    10. supernatural creature   *11. verb*

their pumpkin in exchange for their _____.
                      12. body part

_____ politely declined and continued working. They added
2. name

_____ _____ and a _____ _____ to their creation.
13. number *14. plural noun*   *15. adjective*   *16. noun*

The judges, dressed as _____, began their rounds.
        17. plural Halloween character

When they reached _____'s pumpkin, it unexpectedly began to
      2. name

_____. The crowd gasped in _____. As the pumpkin's
18. verb   *19. emotion*

glow intensified, it projected a _____ light show across the
        20. adjective

night sky. The judges were amazed, and _____ was declared
              2. name

the winner. Their prize? A lifetime supply of candy corn and the title
of Pumpkin Carving Champion.

AD-LIBS

THE CURSE OF THE BLACK CAT

1. NAME_____
2. ADJECTIVE_____
3. SENSATION_____
4. BODY PART_____
5. PLACE_____
6. OCCUPATION_____
7. NUMBER_____
8. PLURAL NOUN_____
9. ADJECTIVE_____
10. VERB, PAST TENSE_____
11. ADJECTIVE_____
12. VERB, PAST TENSE_____
13. ADJECTIVE_____
14. HALLOWEEN CREATURE_____
15. NOUN_____
16. NUMBER_____
17. CONTAINER_____
18. ADJECTIVE_____
19. SKILL_____
20. COLOR_____

THE CURSE OF THE BLACK CAT

On Halloween night, _____ was walking home when a
　　　　　　　　　　　1. name

_____ black cat crossed their path. Suddenly, they felt a
2. adjective

_____ in their _____. _____ realized they
3. sensation　　　　　　　*4. body part*　　　*1. name*

had been cursed!

They rushed to _____, seeking help from the local _____.
　　　　　　　　5. place　　　　　　　　　　　　　　*6. occupation*

The _____ examined _____ and declared they needed
　　6. occupation　　　　　　*1. name*

to find _____ magical _____ before midnight to break
　　　7. number　　　　　*8. plural noun*

the curse.

_____ set off on a _____ quest, searching high and low.
1. name　　　　　　　　　*9. adjective*

They _____ through a _____ graveyard and _____
　　10. verb, past tense　　　　*11. adjective*　　　　*12. verb, past tense*

into a _____ haunted house. Inside, they encountered a
　　　13. adjective

_____ who offered to help in exchange for a _____.
14. Halloween creature　　　　　　　　　　　　　　　*15. noun*

With time running out, _____ managed to collect _____
　　　　　　　　　　　1. name　　　　　　　　　　*16. number*

of the required items. The final object was hidden in a_____
　　　　　　　　　　　　　　　　　　　　　　　　17. container

guarded by a _____ ghost. Using their _____, _____
　　　　　　18. adjective　　　　　　　　*19. skill*　　　*1. name*

outsmarted the ghost and grabbed the last item.

Just as the clock struck midnight, they combined the _____,
　　　　　　　　　　　　　　　　　　　　　　　　　8. plural noun

breaking the curse in a flash of _____ light.
　　　　　　　　　　　　　　20. color

AD-LIBS

THE MYSTERY OF THE DISAPPEARING CANDY

1. NAME_____
2. TYPE OF CANDY_____
3. ADJECTIVE_____
4. HOUSEHOLD ITEM_____
5. STICKY SUBSTANCE_____
6. TIME_____
7. SOUND_____
8. ROOM_____
9. SILLY WEAPON_____
10. ADJECTIVE_____
11. MYTHICAL CREATURE_____
12. BODY PART_____
13. NUMBER_____
14. IMPOSSIBLE THING_____
15. SUPERNATURAL ABILITY_____
16. FAVORITE FOOD_____
17. COLOR_____
18. ADJECTIVE_____
19. ADJECTIVE_____
20. SPOOKY CONSEQUENCE_____

THE MYSTERY OF THE DISAPPEARING CANDY

On Halloween night, _____ noticed their bowl of _____
          1. name   *2. type of candy*

was mysteriously emptying faster than usual. Determined to solve
the case, they set up a _____ trap using a _____
                              3. adjective   *4. household item*

and some _____.
           5. sticky substance

At _____, they heard a_____ coming from the _____.
  6. time   *7. sound*   *8. room*

_____ crept downstairs, armed with a _____. To their
  1. name   *9. silly weapon*

surprise, they discovered a _____ _____ stuffing its
                                10. adjective   *11. mythical creature*

_____ with candy!
 12. body part

The creature, caught red-handed, offered to grant _____
                                                1. name

_____ wishes in exchange for freedom. _____ cleverly
 13. number   *1. name*

wished for _____, _____, and an endless supply of
         14. impossible thing   *15. supernatural ability*

_____.
 16. favorite food

Suddenly, the room filled with _____ smoke. When it cleared,
                                    17. color

the creature was gone, leaving behind a _____ note that read,
                                         18. adjective

"Happy Halloween! Enjoy your _____ wishes, but beware the
                                 19. adjective

_____!"
20. spooky consequence

_____ learned that sometimes the best Halloween treats come
  1. name

with a trick, and vowed to always keep an eye on their candy bowl
in the future.

THE MONSTER UNDER THE BED

1. NAME _____

2. STRANGE SOUND _____

3. HOUSEHOLD OBJECT _____

4. ADJECTIVE _____

5. NUMBER _____

6. COLOR _____

7. EMOTION _____

8. SILLY NAME _____

9. SPOOKY CREATURE _____

10. PLACE IN HOUSE _____

11. EMOTION _____

12. FOOD ITEM _____

13. HALLOWEEN DECORATION _____

14. MUSICAL INSTRUMENT _____

15. ADJECTIVE _____

16. VERB _____

17. VERB, PAST TENSE _____

18. VERB ENDING IN -ING _____

19. PLURAL CANDY _____

20. ADJECTIVE _____

THE MONSTER UNDER THE BED

On Halloween eve, _____ heard a _____ coming from
　　　　　　　　　　1. name　　　　　　　*2. strange sound*
under their bed. Armed with a_____, they cautiously peeked
　　　　　　　　　　　　　　　3. household object
underneath. To their surprise, they found a _____monster with
　　　　　　　　　　　　　　　　　　　4. adjective
_____ eyes and_____ fur, looking rather _____.
　5. number　　　　　　*6. color*　　　　　　　　　*7. emotion*
The monster introduced itself as _____ and explained it was
　　　　　　　　　　　　　　8. silly name
hiding from the _____ that lived in the _____. _____,
　　　　　9. spooky creature　　　*10. place in house*　*1. name*
feeling _____, decided to help. They devised a plan involving
　　11. emotion

_____, _____, and a _____.
　12. food item　*13. Halloween decoration*　*14. musical instrument*
As midnight approached, they set their trap. The _____
　　　　　　　　　　　　　　　　　　　　　9. spooky creature
appeared, lured by the scent of _____. Suddenly, _____
　　　　　　　　　　　　　12. food item　　　　　*1. name*
 played a _____ tune on the _____, causing the creature
　　　　15. adjective　　　　　*14. musical instrument*
to _____ uncontrollably.
　16. verb
Seizing the moment, _____ threw the _____, which
　　　　　　　　8. silly name　　　*13. Halloween decoration*
magically _____ the creature. Victory achieved, _____
　　17. verb, past tense　　　　　　　　　　　　*1. name*
and their new monster friend celebrated by _____ _____
　　　　　　　　　　　　　　　　　18. verb ending in -ing *19. plural candy*
and telling _____ ghost stories until dawn.
　　　　20. adjective

THE ZOMBIE DANCE-OFF

1. SPOOKY PLACE NAME _____

2. NAME _____

3. OCCUPATION _____

4. DANCE STYLE _____

5. ADJECTIVE _____

6. LOCATION _____

7. UNPLEASANT ODOR _____

8. FOOD _____

9. COLOR _____

10. CLOTHING ITEM _____

11. PROP _____

12. TYPE OF MUSIC _____

13. VERB, PAST TENSE _____

14. VERB, PAST TENSE _____

15. SILLY PHRASE _____

16. ADJECTIVE _____

17. FAMOUS PERSON _____

18. EMOTION _____

19. BODY PART _____

20. UNUSUAL FOOD ITEM _____

THE ZOMBIE DANCE-OFF

In the town of _____, the annual Zombie Dance-Off was the
　　　　　　　　　1. spooky place name
highlight of Halloween. _____, a _____ by day and
　　　　　　　　　　　　　2. name　　　　*3. occupation*
zombie enthusiast by night, had been practicing their _____
　　　　　　　　　　　　　　　　　　　　　　　4. dance style
moves for months.

As the _____ full moon rose, zombies from all over gathered
　　　　5. adjective
in the _____. The air was thick with the smell of _____
　　6. location　　　　　　　　　　　　　　　　*7. unpleasant*
odor and _____. _____ arrived wearing a _____
　　　　8. food　　*2. name*　　　　　　　　*9. color*
_____ and carrying a _____.
10. clothing item　　　　　*11. prop*

The competition began with a _____ beat. Zombies _____
　　　　　　　　　　　12. type of music　　　*13. verb, past tense*
and _____ across the dance floor. _____'s signature
　　14. verb, past tense　　　　　　　　　*2. name*
move, the "_____ Shuffle," wowed the _____ judges.
　　　15. silly phrase　　　　　　　　*16. adjective*
In the final round, _____ faced off against _____'s zombie.
　　　　　　　　2. name　　　　　　*17. famous person*
The crowd went _____ as both dancers gave it their all. With a
　　　　　18. emotion
final _____ twist, _____ clinched the victory.
　19. body part　　　*2. name*
The prize? A year's supply of _____ and the coveted Golden
　　　　　　　　　　20. unusual food item
Brain trophy. It was a Halloween night _____ would never
　　　　　　　　　　　　　　　　　2. name
forget - even in the afterlife.

AD-LIBS

THE COSTUME CONFUSION

1. NAME_____

2. ADJECTIVE_____

3. LOCATION_____

4. PROFESSION_____

5. ANIMAL_____

6. COLOR_____

7. HALLOWEEN PROP_____

8. EMOTION_____

9. ANOTHER NAME_____

10. FICTIONAL CHARACTER_____

11. NUMBER_____

12. SPOOKY SONG_____

13. SCARY SOUND_____

14. VERB, PAST TENSE_____

15. OCCUPATION_____

16. PLURAL NOUN_____

17. PLURAL CLOTHING ITEM_____

18. EMOTION_____

19. MAGICAL CREATURE_____

20. ADJECTIVE_____

THE COSTUME CONFUSION

_____ was excited for the _____ Halloween party at
1. Name   *2. adjective*

_____. They had ordered a _____ costume online, but
3. location   *4. profession*

when the package arrived, they found a _____ outfit instead.
5. animal

With no time to get a new costume, _____ reluctantly put on
1. name

the _____ _____ suit. They grabbed their _____
6. color   *5. animal*   *7. Halloween prop*

and headed to the party, feeling _____.
8. emotion

At the entrance, _____ bumped into their friend _____,
1. name   *9. another name*

who was dressed as a _____. Inside, the party was in full
10. fictional character

swing, with _____ guests dancing to_____.
11. number   *12. spooky song*

Suddenly, the lights went out, and a _____ echoed through
13. scary sound

the room. When the lights came back on, everyone's costumes had
_____! _____ was now wearing a _____
14. verb, past tense   *1. name*   *15. occupation*

outfit, while others sported _____ and _____.
16. plural noun   *17. plural clothing item*

The partygoers were _____, but soon realized it was the
18. emotion

work of a _____ playing tricks. They all laughed and
19. magical creature

enjoyed their new _____ looks, making it a Halloween to
20. adjective

remember.

DEAR READER,

THANK YOU FOR CHOOSING AD-LIBS FOR KIDS! WE HOPE IT
BROUGHT LAUGHTER AND CREATIVITY TO YOUR FAMILY TIME.
YOUR FEEDBACK MEANS THE WORLD TO US. IF YOU ENJOYED
THE BOOK, WE WOULD BE GRATEFUL IF YOU COULD LEAVE A
REVIEW ON AMAZON. YOUR THOUGHTS HELP US CREATE EVEN
MORE FUN-FILLED ADVENTURES FOR KIDS EVERYWHERE!

THANK YOU FOR YOUR SUPPORT!

WARM REGARDS,

Made in United States
Troutdale, OR
10/28/2024